This collection of books and ideas belongs to

_____

DATES

FROM_____ TO_____

VOLUME

_____

A GIFT FROM

_____

A Young Reader's Journal

A LIVELY COLLECTION
OF BOOKS AND IDEAS

INVITATION

If you are a dreamer, come in
If you are a dreamer, a wisher, a liar,
a hope-er, a pray-er, a magic bean buyer…
If you are a pretender, come sit by my fire
For we have some flax-golden tales to spin.
Come in!
Come in!

—Shel Silverstein, *Where The Sidewalk Ends*

EDITED BY FRANCIE PAPER
DESIGNED BY PEGGY LAURITSEN DESIGN GROUP

ISBN 0-9650655-6-1

Printed on Recycled Paper

To order copies of *A Young Reader's Journal* or
A Reader's Journal, you
may contact the publisher.
However, try your local book or gift store first.

THE WRITE STYLE
5424 Oaklawn Avenue
Edina, Minnesota 55424
612-928-1962

Dedication

TO MY DAUGHTER, JESSICA,
WITH LOVE.

What I found...is the extreme importance of small
things; how small miracles can make every day sacred.
Small miracles are all around us. We can find them
everywhere—in our homes, in our daily activities,
and hardest to see, in ourselves...

—Sue Bender, *Everyday Sacred*

Table of Contents

I had been my whole life a bell, and never knew it
until at that moment I was lifted and struck.

—Annie Dillard

Acknowledgments

I am grateful to many people—mentors and friends—who freely shared their expertise, talent, insight and support ever since I alluded to the possibility of *A Young Reader's Journal*. I deeply appreciate your gifts.

To Peggy Lauritsen, artist, friend and dream-believer, for translating my words into art and expanding my dreams so they become not only possibilities but realities.

To Francie Paper, editor, mentor and friend, for giving me what no one else ever has—unqualified, unwavering belief and acceptance of my dreams and my Self. I always will treasure your friendship, honesty and wisdom.

To Keith Gaddy Davis, for teaching and learning with me, for believing in me and for making joyful noise at all the right times.

To Shirley and Marshall Besikof, Marlen and Ron Simon, Margie and Marshall Lifson, Caroline and Alex Rodawig, Nancy Held, Shirley Grodnick, Jeannette Kay and Nancy Brown, for grounding me in your friendship, advice and abundant respect. To Pam Abrams, for finding my home, my creative landscape. To Faye and Ralph Stillman, for understanding my adventurous side and for providing me with opportunities. To Jack and Janice Roth, for your personal support. To Janice especially, for your affirmation, inspiration and love of teaching.

To Vicki Lansky, for teaching me, for sharing resources, for letting me trip, fall and learn on my own...and for laughing with me.

To Wayne Raiter, for helping me recover my creativity and for trusting it. Because of our work together, I dream, I search, I wonder, I teach, I laugh and I write.

To Susie and Stephanie Fiterman, for massaging my ideas with contributions I proudly incorporated. To Pamela Holt, Edina Librarian, for your insights regarding the book list.

To Mary Larson and Tracy Constable, for believing that every child is gifted and for encouraging your children to be themselves and to color outside the lines. To Annie Parcels, for your friendship, for inviting me to the cottage, and for sharing your book-loving family with me. To Sara Severson, for letting me raid Danny's book shelves and for your genuine interest in this project. To Marilyn and Clayton Parcels, for the inspiring photo and your generosity.

To my book group friends for spinning stories, weaving ideas and embroidering my life with your friendship.

*W*hat a convenient and delightful world is this world of
books!—if you bring to it not the obligations of the
student, or look upon it as an opiate for idleness, but
enter it rather with the enthusiasm of the adventurer!

—David Grayson

My Wish for Collectors

I learned to love reading as a child. By the time I was seven, the *Bobsey Twins* series, *Nancy Drew Mysteries* and classics like *Little Women* filled the book shelves in my room. When I was hungry for something fresh to read I wandered into my brother's room for a *Hardy Boys* or scanned the shelves of the junior room at my local library. At age thirteen, I was reading the *Reader's Digest Condensed Books* on my parents' book shelves and by fifteen, I buried myself in biographies of painters like Van Gogh and Gauguin as well as great fiction by authors with difficult-to-pronounce names like Dostoyevsky. I felt alive in this world of fascinating characters, imaginative stories, real-life adventures and mysterious places. When I finished reading, I continued thinking, imagining and searching.

When I found other people who loved to read and talk about books, my own pleasure increased. Our discussions were a way of reading the book again, but this time with the benefit of another person's point of view. As they are today, literature classes and book groups became an important part of my life. To capture my ideas about books I'd read, I began writing them down. Once I started, I found it so satisfying I wished that I had begun "collecting my reading thoughts" at a younger age.

Books and my memories of them are treasures. Every book I've read, whether I own it or not, has its own story as well as the one I add from my reading experience. When a friend borrows a book from my library, I lend her not just the book, but the anticipation of our discussion. When she returns it and we chat about the story, she gives me something important—her opinion and her ideas. This exchange energizes me. We think, we question, we debate and often we gain new understanding. Book discussion and writing make me feel like I do after I play tennis, hike a wooded trail or ride my bike real fast.

Collecting and reading are wonderful ways to explore and discover more about yourself and the world around you. This journal invites you to write *your own* reflections and ideas about what you read. Catalog your reading adventures; savor their delights. Spend time with your collection and consider all it opens up to you. What did you learn from this story? How would you have written the ending? What did you like about that character? Who are your favorite authors? Make lists of your favorite books, characters, reading spots, libraries and bookstores.

My wish for you is that you will experience the feelings of a collector. In this journal, you'll find suggestions for "collecting your thoughts" about books. These suggestions may help you get started, but don't let them limit you. I hope you will invent and use some of your own ideas. If you would like to share them with me, I would like to hear from you. Send your reading and writing ideas to:

Margie Adler, The Write Style, 5424 Oaklawn Avenue, Edina, MN 55424

The pleasure of all reading is doubled when one lives with another who shares the same books.

—Katherine Mansfield

Collecting With Your Family

Try these ideas for involving members of your family in reading, writing and discussing books with you.

☼ Schedule a family time for reading a book aloud together. I know this can be difficult because everyone is busy. However, it is worth it and doesn't need to be a long period of time. If you can't do it every day, try to read together once or twice a week. Reading aloud and listening stirs imagination and makes stories come alive. Some readers like to make their own voice sound like the characters in the book. This is exciting for the listeners. Reading aloud to others is an excellent way to read a book that is a little too hard for you to read by yourself.

☼ Build a library of family experience stories. Special events, like picking apples or taking a vacation make wonderful stories. But stories about every day things like making a new friend, helping grandparents with chores or riding a city bus downtown after school are interesting too. Stories worth writing happen to all of us every day.

Family members can write their own stories or you can write a story together. If you are writing your own story and you need help with spelling, ask an adult or someone who is older to spell the words. If you need help with handwriting, ask your helper to write *your own words* exactly as you say them.

If you write a story together as a family, let each person take turns writing the sentences until you're satisfied that the story is finished. Again, be sure that everyone gets to use *their own words*.

Keep your writing materials—paper, pens and markers—handy in a special place. With these, you also may want to have binders, construction paper and a stapler for making book covers.

Clear a space on your bookshelf for *your* "books" and watch your library grow. Share your stories by reading them aloud with your family.

☼ Ask your parents to help you start a parent-child book group. Book groups usually meet regularly, such as once a month. For help organizing and getting started, talk to your local librarian or the owner of your local bookstore. A book group is a fun way to share a common interest and form a lasting bond.

The world isn't made up of atoms; it's made up of stories.

—Muriel Rukeyser

Note to Parents, Teachers & Mentors

I created *A Young Reader's Journal* because of my passion for reading and writing. These passions are so intertwined in my life that I cannot separate them from who I am. They are attached—a part of me, like my arms and legs. Through reading, I seek knowledge and pleasure, exploration and discovery, insight and wisdom. Book group discussion and writing deepen my understanding while they offer outlets for my creativity. Indeed, the more I express myself, the more creative I feel.

I hope this journal helps children to think for themselves, value *their own* thoughts and experience creative freedom. I think writing *their own* ideas in *their own* way will help them to do this. *A Young Reader's Journal* is a tool that will awaken youngsters to the feelings of joy surrounding self-expression.

This journal is intended for children from 9 to 14, or grades 4 through 8 in a wide range of reading levels. Therefore, the book list I selected represents a sampling of the best that children's literature offered within that broad range. The writing suggestions in *Collecting Your Thoughts* are just that—suggestions. They are there to spark ideas, not to limit them. Each child's development and learning style is individual. You and the children may invent many wonderful ways for using this book. I hope you will pursue them and take off in all those directions.

Younger children can use the journal too. They can keep the lists in the *Collector's Treasures* section of the book and, with your help, they can make journal entries. As you help them with the handwriting, be sure to write *their own* words exactly as they say them. In *Collecting With Your Family*, I offer some fun reading and writing activities that can involve the entire family or class. None require a great deal of time, but they do require your commitment. All of these suggestions will engage people, young and old, in opportunities for a lifetime of collecting.

To read a writer is for me not merely to get an idea of what he says, but to go off with him and travel in his company.

—Andre Gide

Collectibles—A Short Book List!

This list of books is a combination of some of my own personal favorites, as well as the suggestions of librarians, reading group experts, teachers, parents and young-reader friends. These authors represent some of the best children's literature offers in a wide range of reading levels. For additional suggestions, ask teachers, librarians, bookstore personnel, other readers or see the books mentioned in the bibliography of this book.

Aesop, *Fables*
Alcott, Louisa May, *Little Women*
Banks, Lynne Reid, *The Indian in the Cupboard*
Barrie, J.M., *Peter Pan*
Baum, Frank L., *The Wizard of Oz*
Blume, Judy, *Are You There, God? It's Me, Margaret*
Brink, Carrie Ryrie, *Caddie Woodlawn*
Bradbury, Ray, *Dandelion Wine*
Bradbury, Ray, *Something Wicked This Way Comes*
Brontë, Emily, *Wuthering Heights*
Brooks, Bruce, *The Moves Make the Man*
Burks, Brian, *Runs With Horses*
Burnett, Frances Hodgson, *The Secret Garden*
Byers, Betsy Cromer, *The Summer of the Swans*
Carroll, Lewis, *Alice's Adventures in Wonderland*
Carroll, Lewis, *Alice Through the Looking Glass*
Carter, Forrest, *The Education of Little Tree*
Chocolate, Debi, *NEATE to the Rescue*
Cleary, Beverly, *Dear Mr Henshaw*
Defoe, Daniel, *Robinson Crusoe*
Fenner, Carol, *Yolanda's Genius*
Fitzhugh, Louise, *Harriet the Spy*
Frank, Anne, *Diary of Anne Frank*
George, Jean Craighead, *A Tarantula in My Purse*
George, Jean Craighead, *Julie of the Wolves* (series)
Golding, William, *Lord of the Flies*

Graham, Kenneth, *The Wind in the Willows*
Hinton, S.E., *Tex*
Jacques, Brian, *Redwall* (series)
Kipling, Rudyard, *The Jungle Book*
Krumgold, Joseph, *And Now Miguel*
L'Engle, Madeline, *A Wrinkle in Time*
Levi, Myron, *Alan and Naomi*
Lewis, C.S., *The Lion, the Witch and the Wardrobe* (Narnia series)
Lindgren, Astrid, *Pippi Longstocking*
Lofting, Hugh, *Dr. Doolittle Stories*
Lowry, Lois, *Number the Stars*
Mayne, William, *Drift*
Milne, A. A., *Winnie-the-Pooh*
Montgomery, L. M., *Anne of Green Gables*
Oz, Amos, *Soumchi*
Paulsen, Gary, *Harrris and Me: A Summer to Remember*
Pyle, Howard, *The Adventures of Robin Hood*
Root, Phillip, *The Listening Silence*
Sharp, Edith Lambert, *Nkwala*
Silverstein, Shel, *A Light in the Attic*
Taylor, Mildred, *Roll of Thunder, Hear My Cry*
Tolkien, J. R. R., *The Hobbitt*
Twain, Mark, *The Adventures of Huckleberry Finn*
Twain, Mark, *The Adventures of Tom Sawyer*
Voigt, Cynthia, *Homecoming*
Wallis, Velma, *Two Old Women*
Wartski, Maureen, *The Face in the Mirror*
White, E.B., *Charlotte's Web*

To know what you prefer, instead of saying Amen
to what the world tells you you ought to prefer, is
to have kept your soul alive.

—Robert Louis Stevenson

Collector's Reflections & Lively Ideas

All of life is a story, and daily each of us collects stories. We share them at the dinner table at the end of the day, with friends or relatives…We live them, we tell them, and we read them.

—Rachel W. Jacobsohn

Collecting Your Thoughts

When you need some help "collecting" your ideas and getting started, ask yourself one of these questions and write your thoughts. Let your mind wander wherever it wants to go. Think and write freely.

1. How does this book relate to my life?

2. Why did I choose this book?

3. What was my favorite part of the book? Why?

4. How does the main character remind me of myself or someone else I know?

5. What did I learn from this book?

6. Is there a place in the story that I would like to visit? Why?

7. How did the book make me feel? What part of the book made me feel that way?

8. Would I like to be one of the characters in the story? Which one and why?

9. What did this story make me think about?

10. How would the book end if I wrote it?

TITLE _____

AUTHOR _____

DATE _____

SOURCE _____

Reflections & Ideas

_____

_____

_____

_____

_____

_____

_____

_____

_____

_____

_____

_____

_____

TITLE _____

AUTHOR _____

DATE _____

SOURCE _____

Reflections & Ideas

_____

_____

_____

_____

_____

_____

_____

_____

_____

_____

_____

_____

_____

_____

_____

TITLE _____

AUTHOR _____

DATE _____

SOURCE _____

Reflections & Ideas

_____

_____

_____

_____

_____

_____

_____

_____

_____

_____

_____

_____

_____

_____

TITLE _____

AUTHOR _____

DATE _____

SOURCE _____

Reflections & Ideas

_____

_____

_____

_____

_____

_____

_____

_____

_____

_____

_____

_____

_____

TITLE _____

AUTHOR _____

DATE _____

SOURCE _____

Reflections & Ideas

_____

_____

_____

_____

_____

_____

_____

_____

_____

_____

_____

_____

_____

_____

_____

_____

_____

TITLE _____

AUTHOR _____

DATE _____

SOURCE _____

Reflections & Ideas

_____

_____

_____

_____

_____

_____

_____

_____

_____

_____

_____

_____

_____

_____

_____

_____

TITLE _____

AUTHOR _____

DATE _____

SOURCE _____

Reflections & Ideas

_____

_____

_____

_____

_____

_____

_____

_____

_____

_____

_____

_____

_____

_____

_____

_____

TITLE _____

AUTHOR _____

DATE _____

SOURCE _____

Reflections & Ideas

_____

_____

_____

_____

_____

_____

_____

_____

_____

_____

_____

_____

_____

_____

_____

_____

TITLE _____

AUTHOR _____

DATE _____

SOURCE _____

Reflections & Ideas

_____

_____

_____

_____

_____

_____

_____

_____

_____

_____

_____

_____

_____

_____

_____

_____

TITLE _____

AUTHOR _____

DATE _____

SOURCE _____

Reflections & Ideas

TITLE _____

AUTHOR _____

DATE _____

SOURCE _____

Reflections & Ideas

_____

_____

_____

_____

_____

_____

_____

_____

_____

_____

_____

_____

_____

TITLE _____

AUTHOR _____

DATE _____

SOURCE _____

Reflections & Ideas

TITLE _____

AUTHOR _____

DATE _____

SOURCE _____

Reflections & Ideas

_____

_____

_____

_____

_____

_____

_____

_____

_____

_____

_____

_____

_____

_____

TITLE _____

AUTHOR _____

DATE _____

SOURCE _____

Reflections & Ideas

_____

_____

_____

_____

_____

_____

_____

_____

_____

_____

_____

_____

_____

TITLE _____

AUTHOR _____

DATE _____

SOURCE _____

Reflections & Ideas

_____

_____

_____

_____

_____

_____

_____

_____

_____

_____

_____

_____

_____

_____

_____

TITLE _____

AUTHOR _____

DATE _____

SOURCE _____

Reflections & ideas

_____

_____

_____

_____

_____

_____

_____

_____

_____

_____

_____

_____

_____

_____

_____

TITLE _____

AUTHOR _____

DATE _____

SOURCE _____

Reflections & ideas

_____

_____

_____

_____

_____

_____

_____

_____

_____

_____

_____

_____

_____

_____

TITLE _____

AUTHOR _____

DATE _____

SOURCE _____

Reflections & Ideas

_____

_____

_____

_____

_____

_____

_____

_____

_____

_____

_____

_____

_____

_____

_____

_____

TITLE _____

AUTHOR _____

DATE _____

SOURCE _____

Reflections & Ideas

_____

_____

_____

_____

_____

_____

_____

_____

_____

_____

_____

_____

_____

TITLE _____

AUTHOR _____

DATE _____

SOURCE _____

Reflections & Ideas

_____

_____

_____

_____

_____

_____

_____

_____

_____

_____

_____

_____

_____

_____

TITLE _____

AUTHOR _____

DATE _____

SOURCE _____

Reflections & Ideas

_____

_____

_____

_____

_____

_____

_____

_____

_____

_____

_____

_____

_____

_____

TITLE _____

AUTHOR _____

DATE _____

SOURCE _____

Reflections & Ideas

_____

_____

_____

_____

_____

_____

_____

_____

_____

_____

_____

_____

_____

_____

_____

TITLE _____

AUTHOR _____

DATE _____

SOURCE _____

Reflections & ideas

_____

_____

_____

_____

_____

_____

_____

_____

_____

_____

_____

_____

_____

_____

_____

TITLE _____

AUTHOR _____

DATE _____

SOURCE _____

Reflections & Ideas

_____

_____

_____

_____

_____

_____

_____

_____

_____

_____

_____

_____

_____

_____

_____

TITLE _____

AUTHOR _____

DATE _____

SOURCE _____

Reflections & Ideas

TITLE _____

AUTHOR _____

DATE _____

SOURCE _____

Reflections & Ideas

_____

_____

_____

_____

_____

_____

_____

_____

_____

_____

_____

_____

_____

_____

_____

_____

_____

TITLE _____

AUTHOR _____

DATE _____

SOURCE _____

Reflections & Ideas

_____

_____

_____

_____

_____

_____

_____

_____

_____

_____

_____

_____

_____

TITLE _____

AUTHOR _____

DATE _____

SOURCE _____

Reflections & Ideas

_____

_____

_____

_____

_____

_____

_____

_____

_____

_____

_____

_____

_____

_____

_____

_____

TITLE _____

AUTHOR _____

DATE _____

SOURCE _____

Reflections & Ideas

_____

_____

_____

_____

_____

_____

_____

_____

_____

_____

_____

_____

_____

_____

_____

TITLE _____

AUTHOR _____

DATE _____

SOURCE _____

Reflections & Ideas

_____

_____

_____

_____

_____

_____

_____

_____

_____

_____

_____

_____

_____

_____

I cannot live without books.

—Thomas Jefferson

Collector's Treasures

*W*hen you give someone a book you're giving them the
most imaginative of gifts, because you're taking a personal
interest in what interests them.

—W.H. Smith

Favorite Books

TITLE   AUTHOR

1. _____   _____

2. _____   _____

3. _____   _____

4. _____   _____

5. _____   _____

6. _____   _____

7. _____   _____

8. _____   _____

9. _____   _____

10. _____   _____

11. _____   _____

12. _____   _____

13. _____   _____

14. _____   _____

15. _____   _____

16. _____   _____

17. _____   _____

I just wrote the kind of books I wanted to read as a child.

—Beverly Cleary

Favorite Authors

NAME   BOOK TITLES

1. _____   _____

2. _____   _____

3. _____   _____

4. _____   _____

5. _____   _____

6. _____   _____

7. _____   _____

8. _____   _____

9. _____   _____

10. _____   _____

11. _____   _____

12. _____   _____

13. _____   _____

14. _____   _____

15. _____   _____

16. _____   _____

17. _____   _____

No human being, as long as he is living,
can be exhausted of his ever changing, ever
moving river of ideas.

—Brenda Ueland

Favorite Characters

CHARACTER'S NAME	BOOK TITLE	AUTHOR
1.		
2.		
3.		
4.		
5.		
6.		
7.		
8.		
9.		
10.		
11.		
12.		
13.		
14.		
15.		
16.		
17.		

*W*e said there wasn't no home like a raft, after all. Other places do seem cramped up and smothery, but a raft don't. You feel mighty free and easy and comfortable on a raft.

—Mark Twain, *Adventures of Huckleberry Finn*

Favorite Settings

SETTING	BOOK TITLE	AUTHOR
1.		
2.		
3.		
4.		
5.		
6.		
7.		
8.		
9.		
10.		
11.		
12.		
13.		
14.		
15.		
16.		
17.		

You can't get a cup of tea large enough or a book
long enough to suit me.

—C.S. Lewis

Favorite Books to Read Aloud

TITLE   AUTHOR

1. _____   _____

2. _____   _____

3. _____   _____

4. _____   _____

5. _____   _____

6. _____   _____

7. _____   _____

8. _____   _____

9. _____   _____

10. _____   _____

11. _____   _____

12. _____   _____

13. _____   _____

14. _____   _____

15. _____   _____

16. _____   _____

17. _____   _____

I should never call myself a booklover, any more
than a people lover: it all depends what's inside them.

—Philip Larkin

Favorite Books to Read Again & Again & Again

TITLE

AUTHOR

1.

2.

3.

4.

5.

6.

7.

8.

9.

10.

11.

12.

13.

14.

15.

16.

17.

*A*ll good and true book-lovers practice the pleasing and improving art of reading in bed. Indeed...no book can be appreciated until it has been slept with and dreamed over.

—Eugene Field

Favorite Places to Curl Up, Stretch Out & Read

1. PLACE

   DESCRIPTION

2. PLACE

   DESCRIPTION

3. PLACE

   DESCRIPTION

4. PLACE

   DESCRIPTION

5. PLACE

   DESCRIPTION

$\mathscr{R}$eading is a means of thinking with another
person's mind: it forces you to stretch your own.

—Charles Scribner Jr.

Favorite Libraries

NAME   PHONE NUMBER

1. _____   _____

2. _____   _____

3. _____   _____

4. _____   _____

5. _____   _____

6. _____   _____

7. _____   _____

8. _____   _____

9. _____   _____

10. _____   _____

11. _____   _____

12. _____   _____

13. _____   _____

14. _____   _____

15. _____   _____

16. _____   _____

17. _____   _____

T he love of learning, the sequestered nooks,
And all the serenity of books.

—Henry Wadsworth Longfellow

Favorite Bookstores

NAME   PHONE NUMBER

1.

2.

3.

4.

5.

6.

7.

8.

9.

10.

11.

12.

13.

14.

15.

16.

17.

Your Own Index

TITLE	AUTHOR	PAGE
1.		
2.		
3.		
4.		
5.		
6.		
7.		
8.		
9.		
10.		
11.		
12.		
13.		
14.		
15.		
16.		
17.		

TITLE	AUTHOR	PAGE
18.		
19.		
20.		
21.		
22.		
23.		
24.		
25.		
26.		
27.		
28.		
29.		
30.		
31.		
32.		
33.		
34.		

We read what we want to know; we write what we want to understand.

—Gloria Steinem

Bibliography

Dodson, Shireen and Teresa Barker, *The Mother-Daughter Book Club*, HarperCollins, 1997.

Jacobsohn, Rachel W., *The Reading Group Handbook*, Hyperion, 1994.

Landsberg, Michele, *Reading for the Love of It*, Prentice Hall, 1987.

Lipson, Eden Ross, *The New York Times Parent's Guide to the Best Books for Children*, Random House, 1988.

Odean, Kathleen, *Great Books for Girls*, Random House, 1997.

ORDER FORM

Please send the following copies of *A Young Reader's Journal* and
A Reader's Journal to:

NAME:_____

ADDRESS:_____

CITY:_____ STATE:_____ ZIP:_____

QUANTITY	DESCRIPTION
_____	***A Young Reader's Journal*** @ $12.95 each
	A Reader's Journal @ $9.95 each *(available in the following backgrounds/colors)*
_____	Abstract Floral/Purple
_____	Abstract Floral/Green
_____	Abstract Floral/Gold
_____	Country Scene/Blue
_____	Country Scene/Copper
_____	Country Scene/Celery

Country Scene   *Abstract Floral*

_____ **TOTAL QTY.** @ $ 9.95 each

_____ **TOTAL QTY.** @ $12.95 each   SUBTOTAL: $ _____

Please add 6.5% sales tax for orders shipped to Minnesota $ _____

SHIPPING:
Book Rate: $2.00 for the first book and $.75 for   S & H: $ _____
    each additional copy (same package)
Priority Mail: $3.00 for mailer plus $.50 handling   **TOTAL:** $ _____

Mail this form with check or money order to:
The Write Style
5424 Oaklawn Ave., Edina MN 55424
Phone/Fax order to: 612-928-1962